Explore Mount Kilimanjaro

Jacquetta Megarry

Rucksack Readers

Explore Mount Kilimanjaro: a Rucksack Reader

First edition published 2001 by Rucksack Readers, Landrick Lodge, Dunblane, FK15 0HY, UK

Telephone   *01786 824 696 (+44 1786 824 696)*

Fax   *01786 825 090 (+44 1786 825 090)*

Website   *www.rucsacs.com*

ISBN 1-898481-10-5   (Rucksack Readers edition)

ISBN 1-898481-11-3   (Explore Worldwide edition)

British Library cataloguing in publication data: a catalogue record for this book is available from the British Library.

Designed by Workhorse Productions (info@workhorse.co.uk)

Reprographics by Digital Imaging, printing by M&M Press Ltd, Glasgow

The maps in this book were created for the purpose by Cartographic Consultants of Edinburgh © 2001

Publisher's note

A walk to extreme altitude involves possible health hazards. These have been explained as clearly as possible, and advice offered on how to minimise them. All information has been checked carefully prior to publication. However, individuals are responsible for their own welfare and safety, and the publisher cannot accept responsibility for any ill-health or injury, however caused.

Explore Mount Kilimanjaro: contents

Introduction

A journey to Mount Kilimanjaro is an exploration, not merely a climb. For some, the appeal is simple: it is the highest mountain on earth whose summit is accessible to any committed walker without technical skills or experience. A well-prepared city-dweller may be able to reach 'the roof of Africa'. This is the allure of the highest free-standing mountain in the world.

However, each walker faces a personal gamble, and the stakes are high: altitude symptoms are unpredictable. No amount of preparation can guarantee success. The only certainty is that everyone who takes up the challenge will reach deep down inside themselves during the ascent.

Reaching the summit is not the only goal: success lies rather in the quality of the attempt. Living a lot closer to nature than you are used to, you will explore your own motivation and recognise your dependency on others. On return from Kilimanjaro, whether you 'succeed' or not, you will know more about yourself, your strengths and weaknesses, and your fellow humans, than when you set out. That's why this book's title begins 'Explore ...' rather than 'Climb' Mount Kilimanjaro.

For anyone interested in the natural world, exploring this mountain is fascinating. In a landscape formed by ice and fire, the ascent takes you from tropical rain forest to arctic conditions among the summit glaciers - contrasts that at sea level would be six thousand miles apart. On Kilimanjaro, you walk from equator to pole in four days.

In temperate latitudes, each season takes months to give way to the next; high on Kilimanjaro, winter drives out summer every night. This is a wild place, full of contrasts and extremes. Plants and animals struggle to survive, in severe conditions of drought, arctic cold and blazing sunshine. Your climb is a journey backwards in time, where life-forms become simpler, species are fewer and the struggle to survive is harder.

The mountain rises over three miles above the plain on which it stands, making it an outstanding landmark. Your journey to Kilimanjaro may become an unforgettable personal landmark in your life.

Planning and preparation

When is the best time of year?

Because Kilimanjaro is so near the equator, the sun is always nearly overhead and the seasons are not as we know them in higher latitudes. The two rainy seasons run from late March to early June and from November to December. It's worth avoiding the poorer visibility and slippery paths in the rain forest if you can. Late June to October and January to early March are the best months to aim for, but remember that heavy rain, snow and thunderstorms can affect mountains at any time.

Another factor to consider is the phase of the moon. You will set off on your summit attempt around midnight, and you may prefer moonlight for this walk. If so, time your trip to overlap with a full moon; see page 63 for details. Finally, decide how much preparation time you need before departure (pages 9-24) and choose a reliable tour operator (see page 62). Aim for flights direct into Kilimanjaro International Airport (JRO), for example via Amsterdam, rather than via Nairobi (NBO) which involves a long ground transfer.

Combining it with other activities

Since the air fare to Tanzania is likely to be a high proportion of your holiday cost, consider the advantages of spending an extra week or more if you can. You could combine Kili with other activities, such as game safaris, a trip to the spice islands of Zanzibar or Pemba, or climbing Mount Meru (see page 6).

If you have a day to spare, don't miss the chance of a game drive in Arusha National Park. It has a wide range of animals, including baboon, wild buffalo, colobus monkey, hippopotamus and is famous for its giraffes (Tanzania's national animal). Bird life is spectacular, ranging from flamingos, secretary birds and eagles through hoopoes and plovers to sunbirds and bee-eaters: you could see 30–40 species in a single visit.

Giraffe, Arusha National Park

The more famous Tanzanian National Parks (Serengeti, Tarangire and Ngorongoro) are much further away, but Amboseli is just across the border in Kenya (see map on page 26). For all but Arusha, you would have to extend your stay beyond one week.

Committed mountain enthusiasts could climb Mount Meru, a classic volcanic cone which stands in Arusha National Park and last erupted in 1893. The standard route to the summit (4566 metres) takes four days and follows the

Kilimanjaro seen from high on Mount Meru

same pattern as Kili, so it makes an ideal preparation. Climb Meru before Kili, allowing a couple of days between the two. The acclimatisation is valuable, and you may be inspired by seeing the sun rise behind Uhuru Peak.

Which route: Marangu or Machame?

Marangu route profile

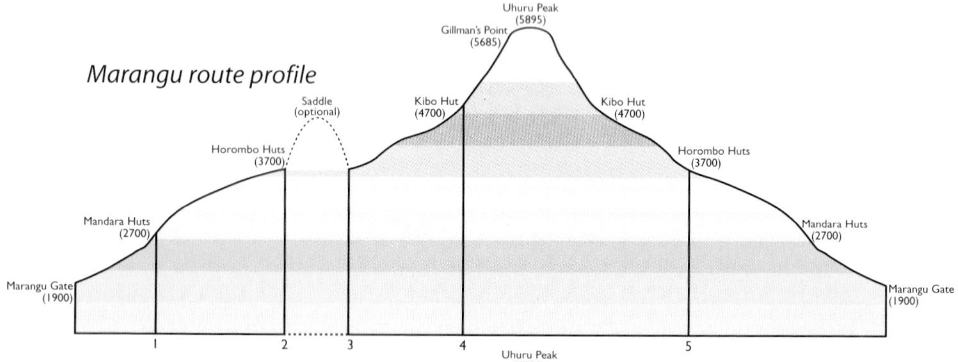

Uhuru Peak (5895)
Gillman's Point (5685)
Saddle (optional)
Kibo Hut (4700)
Kibo Hut (4700)
Horombo Huts (3700)
Horombo Huts (3700)
Mandara Huts (2700)
Mandara Huts (2700)
Marangu Gate (1900)
Marangu Gate (1900)

1 2 3 4 5

Machame route profile

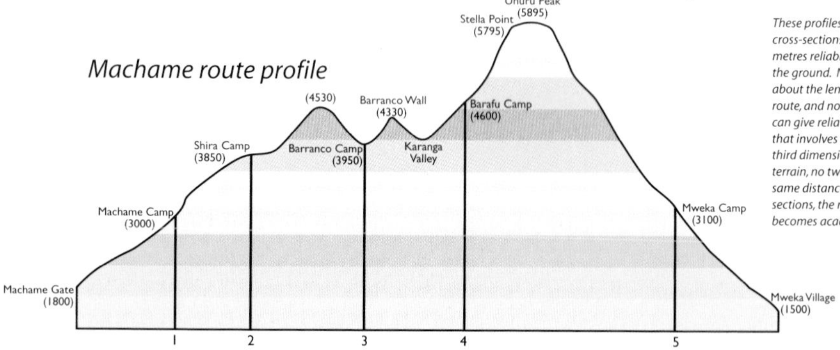

Uhuru Peak (5895)
Stella Point (5795)
(4530)
Barranco Wall (4330)
Barafu Camp (4600)
Shira Camp (3850)
Barranco Camp (3950)
Karanga Valley
Machame Camp (3000)
Mweka Camp (3100)
Machame Gate (1800)
Mweka Village (1500)

1 2 3 4 5

These profiles were created from map cross-sections. They show altitude in metres reliably, but not distances along the ground. No two sources agree about the length in km of the Machame route, and no two-dimensional map can give reliable distances for a route that involves so much movement in the third dimension. On steep, pathless terrain, no two walkers will cover the same distance anyway; in scrambling sections, the notion of distance covered becomes academic.

Although there are dozens of routes up the mountain, the most popular routes for walkers are Marangu and Machame (pronounced Mar**an**goo and Match**am**eh). The route profiles (page 6) and maps (back cover) show how much they differ. They are described in Section 3: the Marangu ascent is in Sections 3.1 to 3.4, Machame ascent in 3.5 to 3.9, whilst Section 3.10 covers both descents.

The Machame route is much more strenuous, because

- you walk further
- you do more climbing and descending en route to your summit attempt
- the terrain is rougher so the walking takes more effort.

Sensible Marangu operators arrange an extra night for acclimatisation at Horombo, offering an optional walk in the 'saddle' region. On this basis, both routes involve five nights on the mountain, but if you are feeling sore or tired, the Marangu route lets you choose how much or little you do on Day 3, whereas on Machame you have no option.

You should also weigh up the accommodation. On Marangu, you sleep in permanent bunk-bedded huts, with solar-powered electricity. Most huts take up to six people, except Kibo Hut which has 60 beds in five dormitories. People of either sex are allocated to huts on arrival. The toilet blocks mostly have running water and are close to the huts.

On Machame route, you sleep normally two to a tent, with only your sleep mat between you and the ground-sheet, relying on your head-torch for lighting. You may find tents colder than the Marangu huts, but you have greater privacy: if you go with a friend or partner you will probably share a tent all week. However, the latrines (toilets) are generally more primitive and further away than on Marangu.

Latrine at Barafu Camp, Machame route

For some people, the choice is easy: if you dislike the idea of tented camping or doubt your ability to complete the more strenuous route, choose Marangu. (It is also called the 'tourist' or 'Coca-Cola' route, because soft drinks and bottled water are on sale in all the huts.) If you regard camping as a bonus, prefer a round trip that lets you see more mountain scenery and are confident of your fitness, choose Machame. If you find the choice difficult, read Part 3 carefully and try to talk to people who have climbed by either route. See page 63 for relevant websites.

At one time, Machame had the advantage of being less crowded, with less litter than Marangu. Recently the authorities were not limiting numbers on Machame, and the route came under intense pressure. On Marangu, the limited sleeping capacity of the huts sets a ceiling on numbers. Weekend departures are the most popular choice, and everybody walks to the same schedule. However at least on Machame the walkers nearly all travel in the same direction.

The Machame route has a reputation for a higher 'success' rate, ie more walkers reaching the summit. Estimates vary widely: overall, the average for Marangu may be only 40-50%, although some operators claim 75% or so, and higher still (80-90%) for Machame. This does *not* mean that you will improve your personal chances by choosing Machame. The percentage is inflated by the number of very fit, experienced hikers who are attracted to the more expensive, more extended route; they are more likely to succeed whichever route they choose. Also, the Marangu figure is depressed by low-budget, minimum-stay tourists who omit the extra night at Horombo – a false economy.

All the evidence is that exertion is a major risk factor in AMS. If your over-riding concern is to maximise your chance of reaching the summit, choose Marangu. It involves less effort overall, and has only one seriously taxing day. On Machame, your summit attempt comes after four full, strenuous days of trekking, and is immediately followed by a longer descent than on Marangu. Reaching the summit, however, is not everything, and there are good reasons why many people prefer the more scenic Machame route.

Sunset over Mawenzi, taken from Barafu Camp, Machame route

Fitness, exercise and heart rate

Muscles get stronger if they are used regularly, at a suitable level and for a sustained period. This is known as the training effect. As a hiker, you might think the most important muscles to train are in your legs, but in fact the heart is even more vital. If you train your heart muscle, it pumps blood more efficiently and delivers more oxygen. Cardiovascular (CV) fitness refers to your heart and circulation: you can improve your CV fitness simply by exercising in your target zone for at least 20 minutes several times a week.

Your target zone

This table shows how your target zone is calculated from your age; the formula does not allow for individual differences. Exercising above your target zone will not increase your CV fitness significantly further, and may tire you faster. Exercising below it will benefit you in weight loss, increasing your power-to-weight ratio. However, it will not noticeably improve your fitness level.

If you exercise within your target zone for 20-40 minutes every other day, within a few weeks you will notice your fitness improving. You will have to work harder to push your heart rate into your target zone, and it will return to normal faster when you ease off. The guideline is to work hard enough to make yourself pant, but not so hard that you cannot also talk. A wrist-worn heart rate monitor takes out the guesswork by showing you a continuous read-out.

Age range (years)	Target zone (beats per minute)
16 – 20	140 – 170
21 – 25	136 – 166
26 – 30	133 – 162
31 – 35	130 – 157
36 – 40	126 – 153
41 – 45	122 – 149
46 – 50	119 – 144
51 – 55	116 – 140
56 – 60	112 – 136
61 – 65	108 – 132
66 – 70	105 – 128
71 – 75	102 – 123
76 – 80	98 – 119

The fit person climbs more easily, uses less oxygen per unit of work done and is more energy-efficient. When everything takes more effort than usual, as at altitude, it helps progress and morale to know that your heart is pumping the available oxygen efficiently to your tissues. Taken to extremes of altitude, your brain is your most important organ: if your judgement is sound, you may take avoiding action before you run into danger.

Unexpectedly, less fit people may be at lower risk of AMS, simply because they are less capable of ascending too quickly. If you are extremely fit, beware of climbing too fast for your body to adjust. However, if you are unfit and/or overweight, you may fail to reach the summit for other reasons, even if you do not suffer from AMS.

Most people already know whether or not they are overweight. Carrying surplus fat adds to your baggage: if you need to shed some fat, do so gradually and well ahead of your trip. This will reduce one risk factor for altitude sickness. However, don't go to extremes: fat insulates your body from cold, and if you are very thin, you will have to carry more clothing to avoid hypothermia, which is another risk factor.

Where and how to exercise

The answer depends on your preference, your lifestyle and where you live. If you live in or near pleasant terrain for walking/jogging, have considerable self-discipline and you don't mind the weather, suitable footwear may be all you need. Consider getting a heart rate monitor to make your training more systematic. Try going out with a friend who also wants to get fit: if your training needs and pace are compatible, you will motivate each other.

If brisk walking or jogging does not appeal, find a mix of activities that you enjoy and can do often enough (three times per week). If you dislike an activity, you won't stick to it. Anything that puts your heart rate into the target zone is fine, eg energetic dancing, cycling or swimming. Consider joining a gym or fitness centre: their equipment is designed to measure and build CV fitness. A gym makes you independent of the weather and limited daylight, there are trained staff and it's easy to monitor your progress.

Avoid relying on a single form of exercise. The smooth flat surface of a treadmill does nothing to prepare your leg muscles for rough terrain or climbing loose scree. If you use a gym for convenience, try to complement it with some hill-walking expeditions in the weeks prior to departure.

However you exercise, minimise the risk of straining your body, especially at first, by warming up slowly beforehand, cooling down afterwards, and stretching both before and after. Stretching beforehand reduces the risk of injury. After exercise, stretching prevents a build-up of lactic acid in your muscles, which would lead to stiffness later. Take a water container and drink plenty before, during and after your sessions.

When and how often to exercise

You don't have to become an exercise junkie to climb this mountain, nor give up your normal life and pleasures. Just get reasonably fit so you can enjoy the experience. Start well in advance: if you are already fit, a month of special training might be enough, but if you are unfit, try to start at least six months in advance. If you smoke, either give it up or at least suspend it until after your trip.

For CV fitness, you need at least 20-minute sessions for maximum training effect, but build up to 30 minutes, and, approaching your departure date, 40-60 minutes. Better still, spend the odd day walking fast on rough or hilly terrain. During the climb your heart rate may exceed the target zone for hours on end, and on summit day you will be hiking for 15 to 18 hours. Prepare your body for sustained effort.

The best frequency for training is every other day: the body needs a rest day to extract maximum benefit from the training session. Since you may miss the odd session, three times per week is the goal for your main training period. In the month prior to departure, build up to longer sessions and higher target heart rates.

Stop training a day or two before you leave, but if you have a spare day on arrival in Tanzania, go for a long walk. Even at only 3000 feet or so, the airport and village of Moshi give many tourists an altitude advantage over their home bases.

Altitude effects

The challenge presented by the highest free-standing mountain on earth is the ascent of over 16,000 feet (5000 metres) in only four days. This section explains the cause of altitude problems and how to prevent or minimise their effects.

This section is based on several books written by experts on high-altitude medicine (page 61), amplified by personal experience and advice from staff at Explore Worldwide Ltd. The books cited are not for the faint-hearted; we have had to simplify and summarise a large technical literature. Here we try to explain the basics and offer practical advice, using a minimum of medical jargon.

How your body responds to lack of oxygen

The altitude problem for your body is the shortage of oxygen. As you climb higher, the air gets thinner. At 5500 metres (18,000 feet) atmospheric pressure is only half of its sea level value. Approaching the summit, each lungful gives you just under half as much oxygen as at sea level, so your body has to work more than twice as hard to maintain the supply.

In simple terms, your heart is the pump that makes your blood circulate. Your lungs load oxygen into your red blood cells for delivery to your muscles, brain and other organs. These tissues cannot work without oxygen. The demand from your muscles depends on their activity level, but your brain needs a surprising amount of oxygen. Despite being only 2% of your body weight, it needs around 15% of its oxygen. If your brain is deprived of oxygen, your judgement declines, movement control suffers and speech becomes confused.

Your body responds in various ways to needing more oxygen. In simple terms:

- you breathe faster and more deeply
- your heart beats faster in order to maintain the oxygen to your tissues
- your body gets rid of excess fluid and creates more red blood cells, making the blood thicker.

You start to breathe faster right away, and your heart rate rises within minutes. It can take several days before your blood starts to thicken: if you suddenly find yourself urinating a lot that may be a sign that your body is acclimatising well. Making more red blood cells is a much longer process that gets under way within a week or two: on normal Kili schedules, this won't be in time to make a difference.

At altitude, breathe deeply and freely as much as possible. Sleep is an important time for the body's adjustment: avoid sleeping pills and alcohol, which depress breathing while asleep.

Be aware that some people have episodes of 'periodic breathing', a pattern in which the sleeper's breathing becomes faster and louder for a minute or two, then decreases or perhaps even stops. The cycle repeats itself, but if the sleeper wakes up with a start, they may be prone to panic. Simply reassure them that all is well and try to get back to sleep. Periodic breathing is normal for some people even at sea level, but it becomes more obvious at altitude; with acclimatisation, it diminishes.

Acute Mountain Sickness (AMS)

Acute Mountain Sickness is what medical people call altitude or mountain sickness; 'acute' simply means that the onset is sudden. AMS symptoms do not last, and, if mild or moderate, may disappear if the victim rests or ascends no further; if they are severe, the victim must descend. Most people who attempt Kilimanjaro have invested a lot of time and money, so the stakes are high. Learn to recognise whether AMS is mild, moderate or severe.

Mild AMS feels like a hangover and can affect people at any altitude above 7000 feet or even lower. Its commonest symptom is a headache (which should respond to aspirin, paracetamol or ibuprofen) combined with at least one of the following:

• feeling sick
• lack of appetite
• difficulty sleeping
• general malaise (feeling lousy, lacking energy).

Moderate AMS differs from mild in that

• there is likely to be vomiting
• the headache does not respond to pain relief
• the victim may be very short of breath even when not exercising (eg after 15 minutes' rest).

Mild AMS is bearable, and affects most people who attempt Kilimanjaro to a greater or lesser extent. Moderate AMS can be seriously unpleasant, and some sufferers have to give up. Although symptoms may clear if there is no further ascent, very few Kilimanjaro trips have the flexibility to allow individuals prolonged rest or to postpone the summit attempt. In practice the choice tends to be simple: continue the ascent or descend.

Severe AMS is different again:

• there is ataxia - the word medical people use to describe loss of muscular co-ordination and balance, as when somebody stumbles, staggers or falls (but see below)
• there may be altered mental states, such as confusion, aggression or withdrawal
• it may lead to fluid leakage into the brain and/or lungs (see *Complications*, below)
• if untreated, it can cause coma followed by death.

However, there are many other causes of ataxia, such as extreme fatigue, hypothermia, dehydration and low blood sugar. Get the suspected victim to have a short rest, a drink, and a snack, and put on extra clothing if need be: this should take care of other possible causes. If they recover promptly, the ascent can continue. If symptoms persist, or if there is mental confusion and/or extreme shortness of breath while at rest, suspect severe AMS.

Severe AMS is avoidable and treatable, but only if you are aware of the possible risks and look out for yourself and others. Most of your group will have mild AMS at some stage of the walk, but anyone with moderate AMS should be monitored closely in case they worsen. Assess the sufferer's condition first thing in the morning: symptoms that persist after resting should be taken seriously. Severe AMS should be treated by immediate descent, oxygen and suitable drugs.

If you are unlucky enough to have moderate to severe AMS, you will probably feel so ill that you no longer care about reaching the summit. Occasionally, because the stakes are so high, some very determined individuals play down or even deny their symptoms and want to struggle on. The problem is that AMS has affected their judgement, and they do not realise how ill they have become. In such cases the guide or group leader may instruct them to descend, and his or her decision is final. If you are on the trip with a friend, you will know that person better than the group leader can, so you can help the decision process.

Over the millennium holiday between 22.12.99 and 5.1.00, 1180 people tried to climb Kilimanjaro: of these 36 had to be rescued, and three died – one from a heart attack, one from a fall and the third from AMS complications. Casualties on this scale are unusual, and could have been prevented if people knew the basic facts about AMS and were truthful about their experiences.

Complications from AMS (HAPE and HACE)

If you and your group act on the advice given so far, you are very unlikely to meet these complications. Edema (spelled *oedema* in Britain) is medical jargon for swelling. Two serious complications are known as HAPE and HACE: High Altitude Pulmonary Edema and High Altitude Cerebral Edema - swelling of tissues in the lungs and brain respectively. HAPE has occurred at altitudes from 8000 feet and HACE from 10,000 feet, although both are less unusual at higher altitudes.

HAPE is caused by fluid from tiny blood vessels leaking into air sacs in the lungs, and affects perhaps 2% of those at altitude, usually people who already have some AMS symptoms. Cold, exercise and dehydration all increase the risk of HAPE. So does gender: men are 5-6 times more likely to be affected than women, and children are more at risk than adults. (Children under 10 years are not allowed above 2700 m (9000 feet) on Kilimanjaro.) Around 1 in 10 HAPE cases will die unless promptly diagnosed and treated – by immediate descent, oxygen and suitable drugs.

The HAPE sufferer looks ill and

- has extreme difficulty in breathing
- is very weak, unable to sustain any exercise
- has a rapid pulse
- may have a fever
- may have bluish-looking lips and fingernail-beds; this is not unusual at altitude, but, if pronounced, is serious
- may have a cough; if any sputum is pink, frothy or contains blood, the case is serious.

HACE is rarer than HAPE, and results from swelling of the blood vessels in the brain: with no room for expansion, pressure builds up and causes ataxia, extreme lack of energy, incoherence, hallucinations or numbness, followed by coma. HACE may be accompanied by HAPE. Unless treated promptly – by immediate descent, oxygen and suitable drugs – HACE can be fatal.

Less serious side-effects of altitude include high altitude edema (swelling of hands, face and ankles) which is twice as common in women. Remove any tight-fitting jewellery before going to altitude. High altitude syncope (fainting) can affect some people who stand up immediately after eating, but they often recover and have no further problems. Some people become prone to nosebleeds; these can be inconvenient but are not serious. Most folk make more intestinal gas at altitude, which can be a harmless source of amusement.

Contact lens wearers may find their lenses become unbearably painful at extreme altitude, and should take spectacles as an alternative. Snow blindness is a troublesome condition that can involve headaches, double vision and acutely painful eyes; choose good quality sunglasses that block at least 99% of the ultraviolet rays and either wrap around or have sidepieces.

How can you tell if AMS will affect you?

You can't. No amount of training, preparation or medication can guarantee future success. You can reduce your risks by following the advice in this and other books. You can take your fitness to new levels, but this will not of itself reduce your chances of suffering AMS.

There is good evidence that things you cannot change, such as age and gender, affect your chances, although doctors cannot explain why. Females are less likely to experience AMS than males. At moderate altitude, young people are more likely to suffer AMS than their elders: the risk decreases with age in an almost straight line. Whether this reflects the greater enthusiasm of youth for rushing up mountains despite warning symptoms, or whether it is a biological effect of ageing, or represents self-selection among the group who climb high, nobody knows.

AMS is highly unpredictable, both in its onset and recovery. On my first trip (Marangu) I was lucky and had no AMS symptoms at any altitude. A year later on Machame, I had mild to moderate AMS on the afternoon of the third day while *descending* to Barranco Camp at 3950 metres. However, I recovered overnight and had no further symptoms, despite climbing a further 2000 metres over the next 24 hours. This is not what the textbooks lead you to expect, but it seems not uncommon on Machame. Other hikers first suffered AMS only on the steep approach to the crater rim, in several cases so badly that they had to turn back.

No expert nor textbook can predict whether or how any one individual will be affected. If you can't face the possibility that you might 'fail' due to AMS, then choose some other mountain.

Does Diamox prevent AMS?

Many drugs have been tried in the treatment and prevention of AMS. The research literature is large and contains some conflicting conclusions. Here we cover only acetazolamide (trade name Diamox), which has been studied thoroughly over 25 years.

Your blood has to maintain a finely tuned balance for bodily functions to work well. When you hyperventilate (pant), as when over-exerting at altitude, you lose a lot of carbon dioxide which can reduce the acidity of your blood. Diamox blocks or slows the enzyme involved in converting carbon dioxide. As a result, it speeds up acclimatisation by stopping the blood from becoming too alkaline and by smoothing out your breathing: it also reduces periodic breathing (page 12). Many people who attempt Kilimanjaro take Diamox with them because it can help to prevent, as well as treat, AMS. Before rushing off to get a doctor's prescription, however, consider the possible side-effects.

Diamox has been known to cause severe allergic reactions in a few individuals. So you should try it out ahead of your trip to test if you are allergic, to experiment with dosage and to discover whether you can tolerate the side-effects which may include:

- increased flow of urine (diuresis)
- numbness or tingling in hands, feet and face
- nausea
- finding that carbonated drinks taste flat.

Since altitude has a diuretic effect anyway, many people prefer to avoid Diamox, wishing to avoid further interruptions to sleep in order to urinate. This may be a problem only when dosage is too high; individuals vary so much that you may have to establish your own dosage: not easy if Kili is your first high-altitude trek. At one time, the recommendation was to take 250 mg three times a day, starting several days before the ascent. Two recent authorities (Houston 1998 and Bezruchka 1994) suggest starting with 125 mg daily at bedtime starting only on the day before ascent, and increasing this to up to 250 mg twice a day *only if need be*.

These dosages are suggested when using Diamox as a preventive measure. In treating AMS, the higher dosages should be used and descent is strongly recommended. Although the medical authorities tend to favour Diamox, I noticed no difference in acclimatisation between the members of two holiday groups according to whether they used the drug. As many people who were taking Diamox suffered symptoms as did those who took nothing. Because of the small numbers involved, this has no scientific validity, but it shows that taking Diamox doesn't necessarily prevent AMS.

Advice on food and drink

Meals are capably provided by support staff and, despite the difficult conditions for preparation and cooking, most people find the food both palatable and plentiful. The diet is rich in carbohydrates, good for helping to overcome altitude symptoms. Bring some snacks and treats such as dried fruit, trail mix, cereal bars or chocolate. They will boost your energy and morale, and can be

Hot food being carried into the mess tent, Shira Camp

shared with others. On the longest day, you may be walking for 15 to 18 hours in all, and snacks help to bridge the long gaps between meals. Bring also some throat sweets or peppermints as many people suffer very dry throats at altitude.

Few people carry sufficient water, and even fewer keep it handy. You dehydrate quickly when walking: every time you breathe out, you lose moisture, especially when the air is cold. Also altitude makes your body produce more urine (the diuretic effect), and you lose water vapour all the time, especially when exercising, as invisible sweat. Expect to drink two to four litres per day on top of the liquid you take with meals.

Try to drink *before* you become thirsty: a water bag or bladder with tube (eg a Platypus) is ideal as it lets you take sips whenever you need without having to stop or fiddle with rucksacks. If in doubt, check the colour of your urine: pale straw colour is fine, but yellow warns that you are dehydrated.

Keep iodine purification drops or tablets in your rucksack, and carefully follow the instructions about standing time and dosage in cold conditions. If the slight flavour bothers you, use neutralising tablets or fruit-flavoured powder. You may want to take some isotonic powder, at least for an extra boost on summit day: this replaces minerals that you lose when sweating a lot.

You can limit your fluid loss through sweating by adjusting your clothing. Try to anticipate your body's heat production. Shed excess layer(s) just before you start to overheat, and restore them just before you start to chill (eg for a rest stop or because the weather changes). Because each of these actions means stopping and fiddling with rucksacks, it's sometimes easier to keep a steady pace and wear clothes designed for flexibility. For example, prefer jackets with underarm zippers and pockets large enough to stow gloves and hat, and trousers with legs that unzip to make shorts.

Beyond the last water point, you have to carry all the water you need. On summit day take care to keep your water bladder or bottle well insulated or close to your body heat; otherwise it will freeze during the night hours. If you use a water bladder, the narrow tube is likely to freeze, so either keep it protected or else blow back the water after each sip so the tube remains empty. Dehydration during the night-time climb is a common mistake.

Summary: how to prevent and manage AMS

- prepare well by becoming fitter (and giving up smoking)
- take suitable supplies and pack your gear for easy retrieval
- avoid over-exertion: if possible ascend slowly enough that you can still breathe through your nose
- avoid sleeping pills and alcohol on the mountain
- eat small amounts of food often, even if you don't feel hungry; avoid excessive salt
- drink plenty of fluids (four to five litres per day), especially water
- if you plan to use Diamox, experiment with dosage well ahead of time, under medical supervision
- do not deny any symptoms you may experience and keep the group leader or guide informed.

Other health issues

Your decision to try to walk to extreme altitude carries risks as well as benefits. Before you commit yourself, talk to your doctor (general practitioner or physician). He or she may have no detailed knowledge of altitude physiology so take along your schedule and route profiles (page 6). Unless your medical history involves special risk factors, your doctor should be enthusiastic about the healthy side-effects of preparing for this trip.

Take this chance to check the latest information on which vaccinations are required and recommended for Tanzania, and over what timetable. Ensure that you store your records safely: you may be refused entry without proof of yellow fever protection, for example. Take advice about anti-malarial drugs and insect repellents (eg something with a high percentage of DEET), and follow it carefully. Malaria is a life-threatening disease which is easy to prevent but difficult to treat. Although for much of the time you will be too high to be at risk, you need protection if only for the beginning and end of your trip; a single infected bite is all it takes.

If you haven't taken anti-malarials before, discuss with your doctor whether you need to take an experimental dose ahead of time. Some can cause side-effects, including nausea and other problems which could be confused with AMS symptoms and generally won't help your attempt. You might want to ask his or her views on Diamox at the same time.

Remember to visit your dentist well before departure. Your feet are about to become the most important part of your body, so consider seeing a chiropodist, and obtain blister prevention and treatment. If you are a blood donor, make your last donation at least eight to ten weeks before you leave. (Your blood probably won't be welcomed until one year after your return, as AIDS is endemic in this part of Africa.)

Upset digestion is not uncommon, so consider what remedies to take, including anti-diarrhoea medicine. Some of those who have to turn back do so because of diarrhoea and consequent dehydration. The nature of the latrines and absence of running water in most campsites makes it crucial to keep yourself clean: take a good supply of wet wipes, preferably medicated.

Finally, the sun's rays are far stronger at altitude, because the thinner air screens out less of the harmful radiation. Since the equatorial sun is already much stronger than most tourists are used to, the risk of sunburn is doubly severe. (On this trip you may risk sunburn and hypothermia within a matter of hours.) Bring a sun hat, cover-up clothing and cream with the highest Sun Protection Factor you can find, minimum of SPF 25 for your face and SPF 33 for your lips, which are especially at risk.

Equipment and packing

There is a packing list on page 24. Major items include a well broken-in pair of walking boots, a suitable day rucksack and kit bag, walking poles and five-season sleeping gear for the very cold nights at altitude. Be sure to test anything you buy specially on weekend walks long before you set off.

Boots

If your walking boots need to be replaced, buy new ones well ahead of time. Take or buy suitable socks and consider buying special insoles (or footbeds). They can make a boot feel more supportive and comfortable, but may need a larger size: a common mistake is to buy boots that are too short. This may lead to serious toe trouble, especially on the way down (Section 3.10). Specialist fitters can fix almost any other boot problem.

Rucksack and kit bag

Your day rucksack should be around 35 litres to hold lots of water and spare clothing. If in doubt, err on the large side, for easier retrieval and packing. Either buy a waterproof cover or liner, or use a bin (garbage) bag.

Check that the rucksack

- is comfortable to wear (test it loaded in the shop)
- has a chest strap as well as a waist strap
- is easy to put on and take off
- has side pockets for small items
- has loops for poles (see below).

Everything that isn't in your rucksack will be in your kit bag, which will spend the week being carried on a porter's head. A suitable kit bag must be large, soft and light, without a frame, wheels or dangling straps. Rucksacks and conventional suitcases are unsuitable: either buy a special bag, preferably waterproof, or use a sailing bag or large sports holdall. It should be tough enough to withstand aeroplane baggage handling (or else must be packed inside something which is).

Support team numbering two porters per hiker, plus guides

Trial packing

Long before you depart, do a trial pack using the kit bag, to find out if you are within target weight (15 kg). Refer to the list on page 24, but leave out your hiking boots, as you will either be wearing them or carrying them in your rucksack. Pack also in your hand baggage anything fragile (torches, sunglasses, camera) and any medicines you might need during the flight, as well as your passport, ticket, vaccination records and other valuables.

If your packed bag is too heavy, try again choosing only the bare necessities. If it weighs under 10 kg, and you have included everything essential, congratulations. Most people will end up with between 10 and 15 kg at the outset, perhaps less by the time the snacks have all been eaten.

Take extra care about packaging and organising: clear polythene zip-lock bags are great for keeping small stuff handy and visible, and cling-film keeps moisture off batteries and other delicate items. Time can be short on the mountain and if you are feeling unwell, you will bless the thought you put into such details.

You will probably leave any surplus kit and valuables at your hotel before you set off for the mountain: this might include spare toiletries, a set of clean clothes, aeroplane reading, personal hi-fi and anything you need for other excursions or parts of your holiday. It is only your mountain kit that must weigh under 15 kg (preferably less). You may be allowed up to 20 kg on the international flight.

Walking poles

Even if you don't normally use poles, consider trying or buying them before this trip. They improve your balance, save effort and reduce knee strain, especially going downhill. Telescopic poles can be set longer for downhill, shorter for uphill. A pair is better for rough, steep terrain, but some people prefer to keep one hand free. Poles can be stowed on your rucksack loops, eg when scrambling. If you are serious about photography, consider the kind which unscrews at the top to form a camera monopod.

Alternatively, you can buy a solid wooden walking stick very cheaply at the mountain gate: made of eucalyptus, they are light, long and strong. However, they would be challenging to bring home on the plane and you may find them less comfortable and effective than the telescopic metal type.

Clothing and night gear

Dress in layers, to help control your body temperature. The base should be a 'wicking' fabric, such as knitted polyester. Over that, wear a medium-weight fleece, eg Polartec. The outer layer is a waterproof jacket and trousers; choose 'breathable' waterproofs that allow sweat to evaporate. Some people need a down-filled jacket in addition, for cold nights at altitude. Pay special attention to good gloves, footwear and head/face protection, to avoid hypothermia and frostbite.

Don't underestimate how cold you may be at nights, especially in tents on Machame. If you can't afford a five-season sleeping-bag and (Machame only) a really good sleeping mat, then borrow or hire them. You can't enjoy your holiday if you are too cold to sleep properly. At higher altitudes, some people need to wear most of their clothes at night, including hat and gloves.

Packing checklist

The checklist on page 24 is divided into essential and desirable. Experienced trekkers may disagree about what belongs in each category, but others may appreciate a starting-point.

You will not see your main kit bag between morning and night: carry in your rucksack everything you need for the day's walk. With the exception of the torches, some spare clothing and sleeping gear, that could mean wearing or carrying everything in the Essential list on most days.

Essential

- well broken-in walking boots
- plenty of good walking socks
- pole(s)
- many layers of suitably warm clothing, including underwear
- hat(s) and/or balaclava for wind and sun protection
- sun protection for eyes and face (sunglasses, high SPF suncream)
- gloves, glove liners and/or warm mittens (especially for summit day)
- waterproof jacket/trousers
- water carrier(s) and water purification tablets
- snacks and throat sweets
- first aid kit including blister, headache and diarrhoea relief
- toilet tissue (biodegradable)
- wet wipes and wash bag equipped for skin and teeth cleaning
- head-torch, pocket torch and spare batteries
- five-season sleeping bag and (if needed) pillow
- warm and comfortable sleeping mat (Machame only)
- enough cash for tips (for guides and porters) plus soft drinks or beer; US dollars are widely welcomed, but take plenty of small notes as you will be given change in Tanzanian shillings.

Desirable

- light and rugged camera; remember spare batteries and film
- waterproof rucksack cover or waterproof liner, eg bin (garbage) bag
- pouch or secure pockets: to keep small items handy but safe
- gaiters (to protect trouser legs on scree and snow)
- thermal sleeping bag liner
- spare shoes (eg trainers or hut slippers), spare bootlaces
- paper and pen, playing cards or book
- guidebook and/or map.

Code for Kilimanjaro explorers

Keep your packaging to a minimum before setting off. Take as little as possible onto the mountain and leave nothing behind except footprints.

Leave no litter: it takes many years to biodegrade, many decades in the dry, cold conditions high on Kilimanjaro. Take your litter with you and dispose of it elsewhere.

Keep local water clean: avoid using pollutants such as detergents in streams or springs. If no toilet facilities are available, make sure you are at least 30 metres away from water resources, and bury your waste.

Don't pick flowers or pull up plants: especially on the upper slopes, plants struggle to survive in extreme conditions and they grow very slowly. Take only photographs.

Book your holiday with operators who put money back into local communities. Prefer those which support Friends of Conservation or like-minded charities.

Learn at least a few words of the local language. Local people will respect and appreciate your efforts.

(Extracted and adapted from the Traveller's Code and reproduced by permission of Friends of Conservation, see page 62)

2.1 Tanzania, history and Kilimanjaro's 'discovery'

Tanzania is a very large country, more than twice the size of California, with many tourist attractions including its Indian Ocean coastal islands and national parks and game reserves covering one-seventh of its area. Its population was approximately 30 million in 1997; most of its workforce of around 12 million are subsistence farmers. The main port and commercial capital is Dar es Salaam, population 1,650,000.

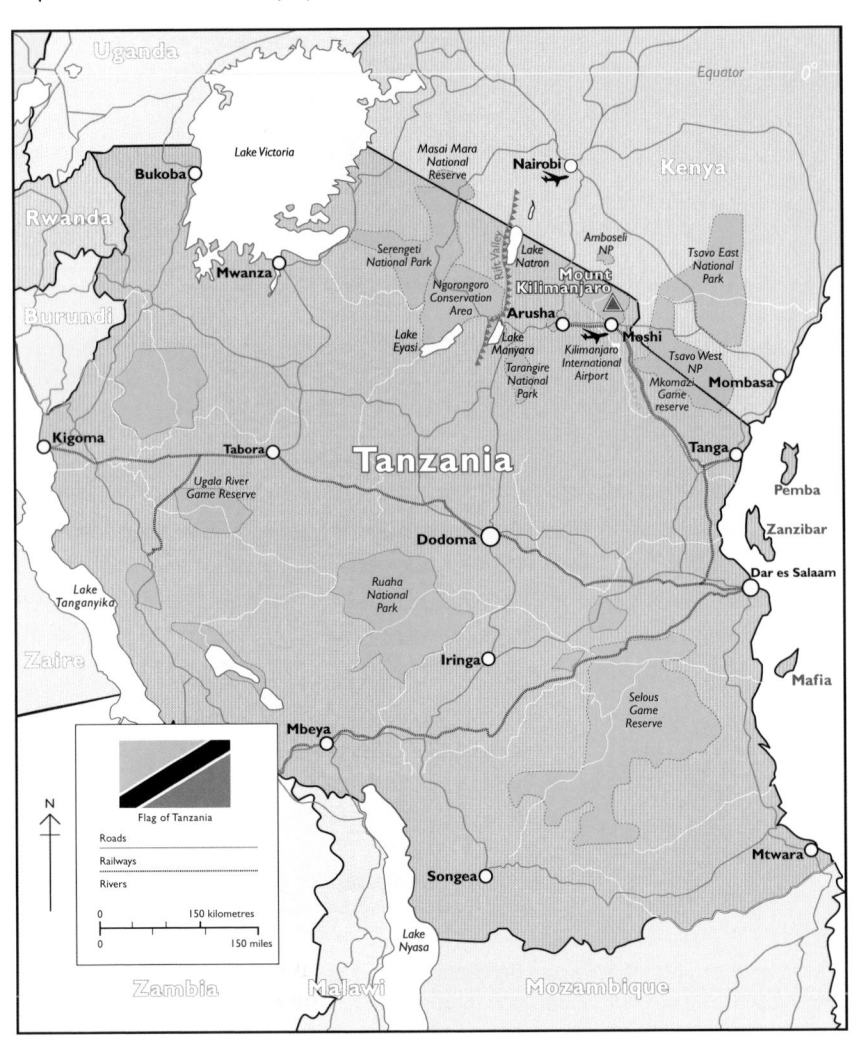

The four colours in its flag symbolise the people (black), the land (green), the sea (blue) and its mineral wealth (gold). The country's motto 'Uhuru na umoja' means 'Freedom and unity' in Swahili, its national language. Tanganyika gained independence in 1961. In 1964 its name changed to the United Republic of Tanzania when it joined with Zanzibar. Julius Nyerere was Tanzania's President from 1962-85.

Mount Kilimanjaro is an important symbol of freedom and appears in the national Emblem. The Uhuru Torch was first lit at its summit in 1961, in the words of Nyerere's famous speech, '[to] shine beyond our borders giving hope where there was despair, love where there was hate, and dignity where before there was only humiliation.'

Although Ptolemy of Alexandria wrote of a 'great snow mountain' in the second century AD, and Kilimanjaro was mentioned by Chinese and Arab writers in the 12th and 13th centuries, Europeans were surprisingly slow to 'discover' and accept the idea of a snow-capped mountain only 3° south of the equator.

In 1848, the missionary Johann Rebmann set out on an expedition to Kilimanjaro, and 'observed something remarkably white on the top of a high mountain'. He soon realised that it was snow, and later identified the twin peaks of Kibo and Mawenzi. He published his account in the *Church Missionary Intelligencer* in April 1849. Bizarrely, the British armchair geographers of the time refused to believe this first-hand account, and it was another 12 years before Rebmann's view was accepted.

Serious attempts by Europeans to climb Kilimanjaro began in 1861, and continued through the 1870s and 1880s, but most groups turned back at the snowline, then around 4000 metres, if not before. Finally, on 5 October 1889, Hans Meyer and Ludwig Purtscheller reached the summit, which they called Kaiser Wilhelm Spitze.

Contrary to a widespread myth, Kilimanjaro was not 'given' by Queen Victoria to her grandson Kaiser Wilhelm. The reason that the straight line of the Tanganyikan border was made to kink southward between the mountain and coast was to place the sea port of Mombasa in Kenya, then British. German East Africa kept the port of Dar es Salaam as part of the carve-up of Africa finally agreed by the European powers in Berlin in 1896.

2.2 Conservation, tourism and the local economy

Hotels in Marangu were running guided ascents of Kili from the 1930s, but visitor numbers were small and grew slowly. In 1959, around 700 tried for the summit, of whom around 50% reached Gillman's Point. In 1997, around 19,500 attempted the walk; by the time you read this, pressure of numbers will have become extreme on both routes, with well over 20,000 walkers per annum.

All land above the 2700 metres contour is included in Kilimanjaro National Park, and the Park regulations are clearly posted. Walking on this unique mountain carries a responsibility to ensure its preservation for future generations. Your Park fees are used to help with maintenance of the trails, huts and campsites, helping the authorities to fight their constant battle against woodcutters, poachers, accidental fire and the scourge of litter. As visitors, we can help in a positive way, not only by never leaving litter, but also by picking up the odd piece we may find on the trail. Follow the Code (page 25) and remember that everyone's behaviour also acts as an example, good or bad, to others.

Exploitation or economic opportunity?

Especially on a first visit to Africa, many Westerners feel uncomfortable about the idea of 'native porters' carrying their baggage and supplies, preparing meals and (on Machame) putting up and breaking down tents. Porters' loads are supposed to weigh less than 18 kilos (Marangu) or 15 kilos (Machame), whereas the average tourist's rucksack probably weighs around five kilos. At one level, this is obviously unfair.

On the other hand, the visitors' holidays pay for the porters' wages, and their tips are an important supplement to low wages. Porters are poorly paid by Western standards, but they are still better off than Tanzanians who are unemployed or subsistence farmers.

Furthermore, after three years' experience, porters may progress to become Assistant Guides, and after a further year or two, reach the rank of Head Guide. Guides are better paid, normally carry only their own equipment, have some training and speak some English.

Both guides and porters are vastly fitter than the visitors, have amazing balance and are well-acclimatised to altitude because of where they live and their frequent experience of ascents. However, they are human, they too feel tired and cold, and occasionally even they experience altitude symptoms. They suffer more from the cold than the better-equipped visitors: porters may have no proper footwear or sleeping bags.

Guides may be better equipped, but because they have to walk at the slow pace of the visitors, they may feel even colder than the porters who are free to set their own pace. Grateful tourists sometimes donate the odd item of clothing or gear at the end of the week, and many Head Guides operate a system for sharing such extras. Such gifts are, of course, no substitute for fair wages and generous tips.

The Chagga people are one of over 100 tribes living in Tanzania. They have lived on and around Kilimanjaro for only three or four centuries, and may have come from the northeast. When Rebmann arrived in 1848 they were divided into over 100 clans, each with its own chief. External force and diplomacy reduced this number progressively to about 50 by 1890 and only 15 when Tanganyika gained independence in 1961. The position of hereditary chief was abolished in 1962.

Most of the guides and porters are Chagga, and many come from the village of Marangu. They are self-employed, within a framework established by the Tanzania National Parks, and they have a reputation for independence and strength of purpose. The missionary legacy is surprisingly strong, and most guides and porters seem to be Lutheran; you may even hear Christian hymns sung in Swahili. They have no name for Kilimanjaro in Swahili, but know its two peaks as Kipoo (Kibo) and Kimawenzi (Mawenzi).

2.3 The volcanoes, geology and scenery

The Great Rift Valley reached its present form only between two and one million years ago. Compared with the earth at around 40 million years old, that makes it fairly recent in geological terms. Long before Kilimanjaro was formed there was a gently rolling plain with the remains of a few eroded mountains. About a million years ago, the plain buckled and slumped, sinking over a period to form a huge basin known as the Kilimanjaro Depression.

The Kilimanjaro of today was formed between 500,000 and 750,000 years ago from three volcanic centres: Kibo was and still is the highest at 5896 metres, connected by its saddle region to Mawenzi (5149 metres). Shira, at 3962 metres, is the oldest and was also the first to collapse and become extinct. Eruptions and lava flow raised Kibo to its maximum height of about 5900 metres some 450,000 years ago, and it has shrunk only slightly since that time. Uhuru Peak, Kibo's 'summit', is simply the highest point of a giant oval crater rim, more than three kilometres long by two kilometres wide.

More recently, the Shira plateau has been worn down by erosion. Weathering has exposed the jagged crags of Mawenzi, formed from slower-cooling, harder rocks that have resisted erosion. Around 100,000 years ago, subsidence caused a huge landslide that breached part of Kibo's crater rim and scoured out the Great Barranco on its way downhill.

Kibo went on being active, and even today it is technically dormant, not extinct. Its most violent eruptions were around 350,000 years ago, producing lava flows up to 50 metres thick. This distinctive black lava filled in the Shira basin and flowed over the saddle area towards Mawenzi.

Kibo viewed from the west, with parasitic cones in left foreground

Later volcanic activity on Kibo formed a smaller crater inside the main one, now known as the Reusch Crater. Over 200 years ago, the last puff of volcanic activity formed the Ash Pit inside the Reusch Crater. Explorers may still find traces of volcanic activity there, but it is not normally accessible to walkers.

Aerial view of the Reusch Crater, with Ash Pit

Kilimanjaro's extraordinary scenery was formed not only by volcanic fire, but also by ice. The ebb and flow of the glaciers has modified the shape of the mountain over hundreds of thousands of years. In extreme glacial times, an unbroken sheet of ice covered the entire mountain down to around 4000 metres, with finger glaciers reaching down to the tree line at 3000 metres.

You might expect that the overhead sun's rays would melt the glaciers, but in fact the flat, white ice reflects most of the radiation. Instead, the dark, dull lava and rocks absorb the heat, and the warm ground undermines the ice cliffs above, creating overhangs and undercuts. As ice blocks fall off and columns splinter, they create shade and help the ground to absorb further heat, melting more ice. You can hear the cracking sounds clearly if you walk past the summit glaciers in suitable conditions.

Kibo's glaciers are in retreat

Sadly, Kibo is gradually losing its ice cap, as is obvious if you compare modern with older photographs, or read accounts of the snow levels in early expeditions. Although global warming may also have a role, geologists have found that Kilimanjaro has a long history of glacial advance and retreat. At times it has been completely ice-free for tens of thousands of years, perhaps because of volcanic activity as well as climatic change. At other times, the ice cover has been so complete that ascent would have been impossible for walkers. So we are fortunate to be able to reach to the crater without technical climbing skills and yet to enjoy the extraordinary beauty of the summit glaciers.

On the Marangu route, in the saddle area you may notice a number of 'parasitic cones': these are small conical hills formed by offshoots of the main lava flow (see photograph on page 30).

Zebra Rock

If you do the optional saddle walk, a mile above Horombo you will pass Zebra Rock, an overhung cliff face marked by light stripes. These were caused by rainwater seeping down the rock-face from above, leaving light deposits on the dark lava.

On the Machame route, you will camp on the Shira Plateau, where there are also many parasitic cones. You will see the Shira Ridge rising 400 metres above the main plateau, with dramatic peaks known as the Cathedral and the Needle. Later you see wonderful views of the Lava Tower and Western Breach Wall, and you walk through the Great Barranco.

Aerial view of Mawenzi (foreground) and Kibo (distance) from the southeast

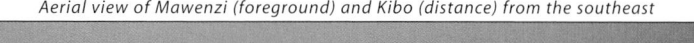

2.4 Habitats and wildlife

Summit

High desert

Heath and moorland

Rain forest

Lower slopes

Uhuru Peak 5895 ▲ — 6000 m

▲ Stella Point 5795

▲ Gillman's Point 5685

5000 m

▲ Kibo Hut 4700

Barafu Camp 4600 ▲

Barranco Camp 3950 ▲ — 4000 m

▲ Shira Camp 3850

▲ Horombo Huts 3700

Mweka Camp 3100 ▲

3000 m

▲ Machame Camp 3000

▲ Mandara Huts 2700

Marangu Gate ▲ 1900

Machame Gate 1800 ▲ — 2000 m

Five zones encircle the mountain for around 1000 metres of altitude, each with its own climate, plant life and animals. The higher you go, the colder it gets and the lower the rainfall, limiting the number of species, and demanding remarkable adaptations for survival.

The lower slopes

The lower slopes range from 800 to 1800 metres, with rainfall varying from 500-1800 mm per year. The Chagga people cultivate the rich volcanic soil, especially on the wetter south and west sides of the mountain. Farming activity has replaced the bush and lowland forest by crops: you may notice maize, coffee and bananas as you are driven past. There are masses of brilliant wild

Coffee plantation

flowers and interesting grasses and clovers. These slopes support a wide range of bird life, including the common bulbul (brown with a black crest), the tropical boubou (a black and white shrike), lots of scruffy brown speckled mousebirds and sunbirds (long curved bills for nectar-feeding and iridescent feathers).

Rain forest

The rain forest occurs between around 1800 and 2800 metres, with rainfall of about 2000 mm per year on the southern slopes, half that to the west and north. This is the source of 96% of all the water on Kilimanjaro, some of it dropping through the forest floor, down through porous rock, to create springs supporting farming on the lower slopes.

Because of the moisture, there is often a band of clouds, mist and high humidity. There are many fine tall trees, often decked with streamers of bearded lichen. Mosses and ferns grow huge in these conditions, and wild flowers include violets, the occasional orchid and the unique red-and-yellow *Impatiens kilimanjari*, which are related to 'busy Lizzies'.

Giant fern

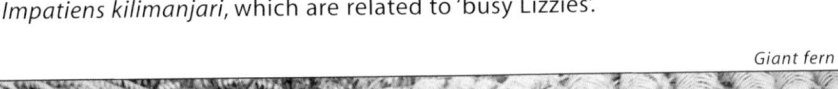

Common tall trees include *Podocarpus milanjianus* (photograph at right) and the huge camphorwoods. An oddity is the lack of bamboo, which would normally occur in the upper belt of rain forest on East African mountains. In the upper forest, you start to see giant heather trees with yellow-flowered hypericum (St John's Wort) growing among them.

If you look carefully, you will see many insects, including beautiful butterflies. Watch out for the shiny brown safari ants, which may bite if you step into their marching column. Fruit trees attract many birds: if you hear a bird braying like a donkey, it is probably a silver-cheeked hornbill (black and white). If you are lucky enough to see a large bird flashing crimson at its wings, it could be a turaco.

Although there are many wild animals, you may not see them since they are shy and easily hidden in the thick vegetation, mist and cloud. You might see blue monkeys (which are actually dark grey and black) and may hear the shy colobus monkeys (black with a flowing white mane) leaping through the trees.

Left: Colobus monkey   *Below: Blue monkey*

Heath and moorland

Between around 2800 and 4000 metres are overlapping zones of heath and moorland, with rainfall averaging about 1300 mm per year on the lower slopes, down to 500 mm on the higher slopes. Above 3000 metres, frost is regular at nights and intense sunshine can leads to high daytime temperatures.

Heather and allied shrubs are well adapted to the conditions: the giant heathers (*Erica arborea*) have tiny leaves and thick trunks. These also occur in the upper forest, where they grow even taller, but heights of up to ten feet or so are common in the heath zone. The varied grasses are important in conserving moisture and retaining the soil.

Three kinds of flowers in this zone are especially striking: *Protea kilimandscharica* is common around Maundi Crater and up to Horombo, but, as its name implies, unique to the mountain. Then there are *Helichrysum*: clumps of everlasting daisy-like flowers of various colours (page 43). Finally, you may be surprised to see huge red-hot pokers (*Kniphofia thomsonii*) standing to attention.

Kniphofia thomsonii

Protea kilimandscharica

The moorland is dominated by giant groundsels (senecios) and lobelias, especially near water courses. Of the various groundsels, the most striking is *Senecio kilimanjari*, which grows into trees of up to 18 feet high. The smaller *Lobelia deckenii* (up to 10 feet) has a hollow stem and spiralling 'leaves' that close over at night. Look carefully inside and you will see their blue flowers sheltering within.

Although there have been sightings of mammals such as elands, duikers and klipspringers, and lions are said to visit the Shira Plateau, the only animals you are likely to see are far smaller: the four-striped grass mouse (*Rhabdomys*

Senecio kilimanjari, probably over a century old

pumilio) has found its niche around the Horombo huts, and is surprisingly tame. If you sit quietly while eating a picnic lunch, you may be approached by the alpine chat (dusky brown bird with white sides to its tail).

Lobelia deckenii

From just above the forest upward, you will often see and hear the harsh croak of the white-necked raven, which scavenges successfully from the huts.
I was once lucky enough to see a Lammergeyer, a large vulture, just above Horombo in the late afternoon.

White-necked raven

High desert

Also known as highland, montane or alpine desert, this zone stretches from 4000 to 5000 metres high and has low precipitation, perhaps 250 mm a year, with summer every day and winter every night. The temperature varies from 35-40°C in the noonday sun to well below freezing every night. Soil is scanty, and what little there is can be affected by *solifluction*: when the ground freezes, it expands and flows, disturbing plant roots. Only the hardiest can survive, and only 55 species are found above 4000 metres.

Lichens are some of the more successful: they do not need soil, but grow directly on the lava rocks. Lichens are a close partnership between fungi and algae. The photograph shows two kinds: red lichen growing flat on the rock surface with grey-green lichen dangling from it; the yellow clump of Helichrysum clings to the thin soil in the rock's shelter.

The tussock grasses are important survivors in this desert, with the mainly dead tussocks retaining moisture and insulating new shoots against the intense cold and radiation. Small insect are mainly flightless, and hide or live underground. Still, they provide a diet for spiders. Ravens and birds of prey visit during the daytime, but cannot live at such altitude.

The summit zone

Above 5000 metres, the air is colder and drier still, and the precipitation falls mainly as snow. There is surprisingly little, probably under 100 mm a year. Rather than falling from above, much of it condenses from clouds sucked up from below when air pressure drops because of the warming effect of the sun. There is no liquid water on the surface: it disappears into porous rock or is locked into ice and snow.

Living things must not only endure the blazing equatorial sun by day, but also arctic conditions by night, when altitude defies latitude. With deep frosts, fierce winds, scarce moisture and less than 50% of the oxygen available at sea level, this environment is deeply hostile to life.

The few lichens that survive are slow-growing: any you see are very old indeed, so treasure them. The highest flowering plant recorded was a small Helichrysum at 5670 metres, down in the crater. Animals are very rare, although in 1926 the Lutheran missionary Richard Reusch found and photographed a leopard frozen in the snow. Hemingway immortalised this animal in his 1938 short story *The Snows of Kilimanjaro* and remarked that 'No one has explained what the leopard was seeking at that altitude'.

The Kersten glacier, seen from the crater rim

3.1 Marangu Gate to Mandara Huts

Time (average)	3–4 hours
Altitude gained	800 metres (2625 feet)
Terrain	mainly good path, may be muddy and slippery during or after rain
Summary	a gentle introductory half-day walking through the rain forest

Tropical rain forest

After your kit has been loaded, you will be driven to the Marangu park gate where formalities are completed (registering passport numbers and paying park fees). From Moshi the drive takes around 45 minutes, and it gains you 1000 metres of altitude: the gate is at 1900 m. Expect the gate formalities to take an hour or two: if you are lucky it may be less. Trying to identify birds, flowers and trees (see Section 2.4) may help to pass the time. Also, make sure you have enough drinking water for the day and a packed lunch.

When you meet your guides and porters, try to remember their names and faces. They are about to become very important people in your life. By the end of the week you may think of them as supermen. (As of 2000, all guides and all but one of the porters were indeed male.)

Unless the path is wet and slippery, this walk may seem disarmingly simple. Maintain a slow, steady pace anyway, to help your body to acclimatise. If you need to leave the trail for any reason, be sure that somebody knows you have done so. If walking as a group, you may stop together for lunch, or even postpone lunch until you arrive at Mandara Huts.

Normally this walk is only a half-day, and there is plenty of time to visit Maundi Crater, a 15-minute walk from Mandara. The extra effort is rewarded by brilliant wild flowers and perhaps superb views of Kibo and Mawenzi.

Mandara Huts with (inset) white-necked raven perching on hut

3.2 Mandara Huts to Horombo Huts

Time (average)	**5-6 hours**
Altitude gained	**1000 metres (3280 feet)**
Terrain	**good footpath with steady gradients**
Summary	**after clearing the forest, you walk across moorland with some great open views**

After an early breakfast, you will start the day's walk by clearing the forest and perhaps seeing more views of Kibo and Mawenzi. The vegetation is changing markedly now, and at your picnic lunch (usually at the halfway point) you may see the four-striped grass mice, which are keen scavengers.

If it is clear, you will be enjoying mountain views for much of this day's walk, on a good footpath. You may well arrive at Horombo by early to mid-afternoon. If your group is spending an acclimatisation day, you will have two nights here, probably in the same hut (but leave your gear stowed tidily, just in case). Dinner, as at Mandara, is served in the communal dining hut by the support team.

Horombo Huts

Clump of Helichrysum ('Everlastings')

On an acclimatisation day, the saddle walk to the north is highly recommended: the views of Kibo and Mawenzi are terrific, the ascent and descent (from 3700 to 4400 m and back) is just what your body needs, and if you set off early you will still have most of a free afternoon. You will also be able to see Middle Red, West Lava and East Lava Hills, as well as Barafu Camp to the west. However, if you are nursing blisters or other problems you can opt out of the walk, or do it in part, to suit your energy level. At the very least, visit Zebra Rock, only a mile or so above Horombo (see page 32).

From the saddle area, note the steep path to Gillman's Point (right)

3.3 Horombo Huts to Kibo Hut

Time (average)	**5-6 hours**
Altitude gained	**1000 metres (3280 feet)**
Terrain	**good path with steady gradients easing across the saddle (middle of the day)**
Summary	**passing through high semi-desert, you see some good views of Mawenzi and Kibo**

The first part is similar to the optional saddle walk but the path bears off at a more north-westerly angle. Approaching the high desert of the saddle region, notice how the giant groundsel (senecios, see page 37) persist wherever there is a watercourse. Top up your water supplies at the Last Water point (1.5 to 2 hours above Horombo Hut). The path steepens, and the landscape becomes even bleaker, as you approach Kibo Hut.

Giant senecio and heather (foreground), Mawenzi (background)

You may arrive at Kibo Hut by early afternoon for a well-earned rest before the major challenge of the night's summit attempt. Make sure that you purify (or buy) plenty of drinking water for the night's walk, and pack it so your body warmth reaches the water, otherwise it will freeze. The most common mistake people make at altitude is not drinking enough.

This is also the moment to insert fresh batteries and film in your camera and to check or replace your head-torch battery. Pack enough snacks and morale boosters to see you through the night's walking, arrange your warmest clothing ready for action, including gloves, hat and thermals. Then put your head down and sleep for as long as you can. If you cannot sleep, just relax and think peaceful thoughts: your body needs to rest before the very strenuous 24 hours ahead.

High desert, approaching Kibo Hut, with Mawenzi (background)

Horombo Huts   1000   Kibo Hut

3.4 Kibo Hut to Gillman's Point/Uhuru Peak

Time (average)	**6-10 hours**
Altitude gained	**985/1195 metres (3230/3920 feet) to Gillman's Point/ Uhuru**
Terrain	**a steep, rough ascent on loose scree and rocks to the crater rim; gentler gradients thereafter**
Summary	**by far the most strenuous stage of the route, normally attempted between midnight and dawn**

You will be woken around midnight to walk through the night. This is mainly because you need the time to try to reach the summit and still be able to descend in daylight. To reach your next night's accommodation via Uhuru, you need not only to gain 1195 metres of vertical height, on a slope averaging some 27%, but also to lose 2195 metres (Section 3.10). Also, in some ways walking at night is easier as the scree is firmer when cold or frozen and the snow less slushy in the early morning.

Sunrise behind Mawenzi, summit ascent

On waking, slip into as many layers of clothing as you have: you will be cold, perhaps very cold, to start with, but may need to shed layers after you have been climbing for a while. Alternatively, if a high wind gets up, you may become colder than ever, especially your hands, feet and ears.

Eat and drink whatever is on offer. Check that your drinking water and snacks are handy and that the water will not freeze. When your head-torch is switched on, take care not to dazzle others by looking directly at them. If there is moonlight, you may not need the head-torch.

The first half of this ascent is on a steep, winding rocky path. Try to maintain a very slow, but steady pace: this may be less tiring than constantly stopping for short pauses. Shorten your stride if need be, and don't be afraid to hang back if the pace is too fast for you. Many people get into a trance-like rhythm, trudging up rhythmically through the starlight. The halfway point is Hans Meyer Cave (5150 metres) where you may have a slightly longer rest.

After the Cave, the path becomes steeper as it zig-zags up towards Gillman's Point. This is by far the most difficult section of the route: just plod on, don't be discouraged by the way that Gillman's Point mysteriously seems to recede. If you are determined enough, and escape altitude sickness, you will get there in the end. If your feet slip back on the scree, try pushing harder on those poles, and edge in with your boots. As you near or

Summit glacier seen from crater rim

reach the crater rim, the sun will raise your morale and body temperature. Pause to enjoy what is generally considered the finest sunrise on earth.

From Gillman's Point, it takes another 1.5 to 2 hours to Uhuru Peak, although the gradients are much gentler and the terrain easier. There's no point in making a colossal effort to reach the summit unless you are also still capable of getting yourself down: read Section 3.10 carefully ahead of time. You may find that the achievement of reaching the summit gives you a rush of energy that sees you through this, perhaps the longest day of your life.

3.5 Machame Gate to Machame Camp

Time (average)	5-7 hours
Altitude gained	1200 metres (3940 feet)
Terrain	rough path with many tree roots; very slippery and muddy when wet
Summary	a straightforward first day, unless wet underfoot, on a path enclosed by rain forest

As with the Marangu route, the day begins with a drive to the park gate (Machame) and the formalities (registering passport numbers and paying park fees) take an hour or two. From Moshi the drive takes about 35 minutes, and it takes you to 1800 metres. Trying to identify birds, flowers and trees (see Section 2.4) may help you to pass the time. Also, make sure you have enough drinking water for the day and a packed lunch.

When you meet your guides and porters, try to remember their names and faces. They are about to become very important people in your life. By the end of the week you may think of them as supermen. Because the terrain is rough and sometimes steep, on this route porters occasionally fall. Even with your lighter load and poles for support, you may on occasion struggle for balance, especially if it is wet and muddy underfoot. Spare a thought for the people who are carrying your luggage, tents and cooking equipment.

The walk through the rain forest is full of interest, although it feels curiously enclosed for a mountainside. Mist and cloud are common in the late morning to mid-afternoon, and on arrival at Machame Camp you may see disappointingly little. Early mornings are better for views at this height. Get in the habit of looking around the campsite and locating your torch well before darkness falls.

Machame Camp

Machame Gate   1200   Machame Camp

3.6 Machame Camp to Shira Camp

Time (average)	**5-7 hours**
Altitude gained	**850 metres (2790 feet)**
Terrain	**path mostly good with only one real scramble – the rocky ridge leading to Shira plateau**
Summary	**steady climb leads to splendid campsite on Shira plateau**

After an early breakfast, you set off toward Shira plateau. Leaving the forest, the path heads up into the moorland along a ridge of volcanic rock. About two hours after Machame, there is a short scramble up a rock 'wall', but this is not very challenging (American Class 3, British grade 1) nor high (about 8 metres). The path climbs steadily along the ridge towards a picnic lunch stop, usually at around 3600 metres.

Once you have completed the rocky ridge, you head north, apparently away from Kibo. After crossing some streams, you emerge on to Shira plateau, where the gradients ease and you pass Shira Cave. Shira is the oldest of the three volcanoes that make up the Kilimanjaro massif, and its plateau has many interesting features and minerals. You may notice shiny jet black pebbles lying on the ground: they are made of obsidian.

Continuing north, you soon reach the first of three campsites. From here you may have splendid views of the Shira Ridge to the west, with its three pinnacles of Shira Needle, Shira Cathedral and East Shira Hill. Looking east, you may see Kibo's Western Breach and its glaciers. Far away, to the south west, you might even see Mount Meru (page 6).

Shira Camp

Machame Camp   850   Shira Camp

3.7 Shira Camp to Barranco Camp

Time (average)	**5–6 hours**
Altitude gained	**rising 680 metres (2230 feet) above Shira before steep descent to camp (100 m/330 ft net gain)**
Terrain	**fairly rough path, some scree, some steep sections**
Summary	**through rocky semi-desert with dramatic views of the Lava Tower and Breach Wall**

From Shira, your route turns sharply east, and at last you are walking directly toward Kibo and its Western Breach. The line of nearby hills to the left of Kibo is the Oehler Ridge. You climb steadily to a high point of 4530 metres (14,860 feet), close to the distinctive Lava Tower. There are impressive cliffs and rock formations all the way, with some interesting colours if the light is good.

Breaking up Shira Camp

The last few hours of the day are spent descending steeply into the Great Barranco (valley), ending at an altitude of 3950 metres, only 100 metres higher than your starting-point. Nevertheless, you will have climbed and descended 680 metres (2230 feet) and may be ready for a hard-earned night's sleep. First, take time to enjoy the spectacular situation of Barranco Camp. It lies below the Western Breach; the front cover photograph was taken from here.

Lava Tower

Shira Camp — 680 — Barranco Camp

3.8 Barranco Camp to Barafu Camp

Time (average)	**7–8 hours**
Altitude gained	**rises 380 metres (1250 feet) over the Barranco Wall, then falls and rises to Barafu (650 m/2130 ft net gain)**
Terrain	**after a steep, exposed climb up the Barranco Wall (some scrambling), gradients ease**
Summary	**a taxing day, to be followed by an even tougher night, but with good views**

From the campsite, you head north for a short distance and cross a river before meeting the day's main challenge: the imposing-looking Barranco Wall. Although the Wall is close to vertical in places, your route takes a diagonal line and is less difficult than it looks; still this is a stiff climb of over 300 metres. The scrambling is no more difficult than on Day One, but it is more exposed and lasts much longer. You will feel a great sense of achievement looking down from the top.

If you aren't used to scrambling, follow behind someone who is, putting your hands where he or she does: your feet will follow. If you are worried by the exposure, don't look down. Think of the Wall as a long, uneven staircase with the odd section of rope ladder. Take comfort from the fact that, unlike the porters, you have your hands free and you're carrying a lot less weight.

After the Wall, the path crosses a plateau area divided by several valleys with superb views up towards the southern icefields (Heim, Kersten and Decken glaciers, in the order that you see them). You descend fairly steeply into the Karanga Valley (4000 m), where most groups stop for lunch and which is the last water point. Water must be carried from here to Barafu campsite and onward. You may be lucky enough to have a cooked lunch al fresco, providing fuel for your night-time attempt on the summit.

Hot lunch, Karanga Valley

About 3 km after the Karanga Valley, the circuit path meets the Mweka trail, which is the normal Machame descent route. You turn left at this junction, heading up toward Barafu Camp. Alternatively, your group may take a more diagonal route from Karanga Valley, in effect cutting the corner to reach Barafu. Once you are settled in, watch out for lovely evening light on Mawenzi: the back cover photograph was taken here near sunset.

As the campsite is exposed and rocky, it is especially important to familiarise yourself with the terrain before dark falls. There have been a number of accidents at Barafu over the years, mainly at night. Read also page 45 for reminders on checking your gear before nightfall.

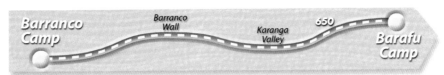
Barranco Camp — Barranco Wall — Karanga Valley — 650 — Barafu Camp

3.9 Barafu Camp to Stella Point/Uhuru Peak

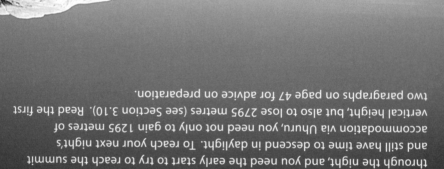

Time (average)	6–10 hours
Altitude gained	1195/1295 metres (3920/4250 feet) to Stella Point/Uhuru
Terrain	a steep, rough ascent on loose scree and rocks to the crater rim; more gradual thereafter
Summary	the most strenuous stage of a strenuous route, normally attempted between midnight and dawn

As on the Marangu route, you will be woken around midnight to walk through the night, and you need the early start to try to reach the summit and still have time to descend in daylight. To reach your next night's accommodation via Uhuru, you need not only to gain 1295 metres of vertical height, but also to lose 2795 metres (see Section 3.10). Read the first two paragraphs on page 47 for advice on preparation.

The steep climb to Stella Point takes you past the Rebmann glacier

Most people find the climb to Stella Point the most daunting section of the Machame route, mainly because of the dark and the altitude. However, it presents no technical difficulties. It is a long steep slog, very steep in places, but if you are determined and escape altitude sickness, you will get there in the end. If your feet slip back on the scree, try pushing harder on those poles and edge in with your boots; watch the guides. As you near or reach Stella Point, the sunrise will raise your morale and body temperature (see photograph on page 46).

From Stella Point it takes another three-quarters to one hour to Uhuru Peak, although the gradients are much gentler and the terrain easier. There's no point in making a superhuman effort to reach the summit unless you are also still capable of getting yourself down: read Section 3.10 carefully ahead of time. However, you may find that the achievement of reaching the summit gives you a rush of energy that sees you through this, perhaps the longest day of your life.

3.10 The summit day descent

Time (average)	**4-8 hours (including rest/lunch stop)**
Altitude lost	**from Uhuru, 2195 metres (7200 feet) to Horombo or 2795 metres (9170 feet) to Mweka**
Terrain	**gradual descent around crater rim, then steep, loose scree followed by rough path**
Summary	**many people find the descent hard on the knees and feet: don't underestimate this stage**

This is the second part of the summit day that began at midnight with the eerie climb towards the crater rim in the dark. Coming down sounds simple, and most people underestimate it; some books don't mention this stage at all. However, your chances of falling are always greater on the way down a mountain, and on the steep scree of Kilimanjaro, they are higher than usual. Older walkers will realise that descent can be harder than ascent, with potential damage to knees and toes.

The figures are impressive: from Uhuru, you need to lose 2195 metres of altitude to reach Horombo (on Marangu) or 2795 metres to reach Mweka (on Machame). Even from the crater rim, you have to lose 1985 or 2695 metres respectively. These are serious descents, probably further than you could ever attempt on a day walk at home. Your body has to perform this task immediately after a night of unprecedented exertion at altitude with no sleep.

Walkers descending towards Kibo Hut (centre)

Then there's the terrain: although the crater rim walk is fairly straightforward, the steep scree is another matter. You may be especially glad of two poles at this point. The guides have a nifty technique of half-running and half-sliding down the scree: some people copy this easily, others fall a lot. If you fall, try to relax on the way down and watch out for rocks. Don't let yourself be pressurised into descending faster than you want to. The dust may create a serious problem for your eyes, nose and throat. Either protect your face or hang back (or both): the problem is worst when you follow another walker closely.

However you come down, your knees and toes may find it hard going. Before you start, make sure your boots are tightly laced over the instep: the goal is to prevent your toes from hitting against the end of the boot. This can cause lasting numbness, especially in the big toe, and may lead to later loss of a toenail or two. If your boots were not long enough in the first place, you will find this out to your cost.

Once safely down, you will find beer on sale at Horombo Hut or Mweka Camp. By all means enjoy one or two, but be aware that you are still at high altitude (3700 or 3100 metres) and alcohol will have around double its sea-level effect. It is also a diuretic, and may reduce your chances of an unbroken night's sleep.

The final day on the mountain is not described separately. On the Marangu route, it is a repeat of the first two days' climb in reverse (1800 metres from Horombo to Marangu Gate), with a lunch stop probably at Mandara Huts. On the Mweka route, it is a shorter descent (1600 metres from Mweka Camp to Mweka Gate) mainly through the rain forest. You may be carrying a picnic lunch to eat en route or at Mweka Gate.

Your last day on the mountain is precious; with the pressure off, it seems a shame to hurry it. However, remember that you will be saying goodbye to the guides and porters at the park gate. They will be given their hard-earned tips before returning to their families, and you will not want to delay them unduly. If you are lucky, they may even sing for you – giving you a lasting memory of an unforgettable week.

Sunset over Kibo

Reference

Get by in Swahili

hello	jambo
goodbye	kwaheri
thank you (very much)	asante (sana)
welcome	karibu
no problem	hakuna matata
sorry	pole
slowly	pole pole
quickly	haraka
let's go (now)	twende (sasa)
yes	ndiyo
no	hapana
danger	hatari
help	usaidizi
toilet	choo
water (drinking)	maji (ya kunywa)
journey	safari
I am tired	nimechoka
my head aches	kichwa kinauma
I feel (much) better	afadhali (sana)
fine, good (very good)	mzuri (sana)
bad	mbaya
hungry	njaa
thirsty	kiu
expensive	ghali
cheap	rahisi
ice, hail	barafu
storm	kipunga
how are things?	habari?
how much/many?	ngapi?
where?	wapi?
when?	lini?
why?	kwa-nini?

Further reading

Bezruchka, Stephen *Altitude Illness: Prevention and Treatment* Cordee 1994 ISBN 1-871890-57-8

Pocket-sized 93-page coverage of the causes, symptoms and signs, with decision trees, tables and interesting case studies; good index but no glossary

Houston, Charles *Going Higher: Oxygen, Man and Mountains* Swan Hill Press, 1998 ISBN 1-84037-097-1

Substantial (272-page) treatment of atmospheric oxygen, mountain sickness and its prevention and treatment; case studies, line drawings and glossary help the non-medical reader, but still not easy reading in places; long bibliography underlines its authoritative status

There are also many websites with information on AMS, but some are unreliable; the above books are recommended.

For technical climbing on Kili, a good source (with excellent bibliography) is: Burns, Cameron *Kilimanjaro & Mount Kenya: A Climbing and Trekking Guide* Cordee 1998 ISBN 1-87189-98-5

Rucksack Readers

The author/publisher welcomes feedback on this book and ideas for future editions and further titles. Within reason, we can offer further advice and information about Kili to readers by email. If there is demand, we may establish an online conference or FAQ page, so please check our website (which also covers other long-distance walking titles) before emailing.

website: www.rucsacs.com
email: info@rucsacs.com

Landrick Lodge, Dunblane, FK15 0HY, UK
Tel: +44 (0) 1786 824 696
Fax: +44 (0) 1786 825 090

Contact details

To phone UK numbers from outside the UK, dial the access code followed by the number as shown, ignoring the leading zero (0). Within the UK, ignore the +44 and dial the 0 instead.

NB This section was checked prior to publication, but phone numbers and website addresses are liable to change without notice.

Explore Worldwide

This company, established in 1981, specialises in small group exploratory holidays and has been running trips to Kilimanjaro (Marangu and Machame) since 1993. Its UK Head Office details are given below, and it also has offices in six other European countries, Australia, Canada, Hong Kong, USA, New Zealand, and South Africa: check the Explore website for details.

Explore Worldwide Ltd
1 Frederick Street
Aldershot, Hants
GU11 1LQ
UK
Tel: +44 (0) 1252 760 100

website: www.exploreworldwide.com
email: info@exploreworldwide.com

Ground agents

Shah Tours is a specialist local operator of Kilimanjaro treks, covering all routes since 1985.

Shah Tours & Travels Ltd
PO Box 1821
Moshi
Tanzania
Tel: 00 255 27 275 2998
Fax: 00 255 27 275 1449

website: www.kilimanjaro-shah.com
email: kilimanjaro@eoltz.com

Kearsley Travel & Tours is a long-established ground operator of Tanzanian safaris.

Kearsley Travel & Tours
PO Box 801
Dar es Salaam
Tanzania
Tel: 00 255 22 211 5026
Fax: 00 255 22 211 5585

website: www.kearsley.net
email: kearsley@raha.com

Friends of Conservation

FoC was founded in 1982 to promote a balance between tourists enjoying their trips abroad and conservation of the local environments which they visit. FoC works with local peoples to encourage a balance between their needs and those of the wildlife with which they share habitats and ecosystems, and it publishes the Traveller's Code (see extract, page 25). It is supported by a number of responsible travel operators and by individual membership (UK Registered Charity 328176).

Friends of Conservation
Riverbank House
1 Putney Bridge Approach
London
SW6 3JD UK
Tel   +44 (0) 207 731 7803
website: www.foc-uk.com
email: info@foc-uk.com

Tanzania

Most visitors need a visa for admission to Tanzania. Britons should apply to the Tanzanian High Commission, 43 Hertford St, London, W1Y 8DB. American citizens should apply to the Tanzanian Embassy in Washington and others should seek advice from their travel agent or tour operator. There is a useful country profile on this website: www.tanzania-online.gov.uk (email for visa enquiries is visa@tanzania-online.gov.uk).

Kilimanjaro websites

It is worth searching online using your favourite search engine: if you narrow the search by route, you will still typically find thousands of hits each for "Marangu" and "Machame". Websites may not be maintained or updated in future years, but as of December 2000, the following selection (in no particular order) were working and worth visiting:

www.web.netactive.co.za/~gdebeer/kiliIntro.html

www.rose-hulman.edu/~waitel/intro.html

www.calle.com/~carl/kilisaver/slideindex.html

www.gorp.com/gorp/location/africa/tanzania/home_kil.htm

www.demis.nl/poul/Kilimanjaro_in_december.htm

www.climb.co.za/kilimachame.htm

www.globalserve.net/~wallace1/quatern/webpres/kilimanjaro.html

Star-gazing

Because the nights are truly black and the air is thin, from Kilimanjaro the stars look unexpectedly brilliant. If you are familiar with constellations at home, you will find that near the equator they appear at an unfamiliar angle and appear to move differently. A helpful website has been created especially for readers of this book, and is highly recommended:

www.digitalbrain.com/user/Kilimanjaro/public/Kilimanjaro

Full moon

You will find the dates of each full moon in the current year in many pocket diaries and in any almanack. When full, the moon looks the same from anywhere on earth, although in its other phases the crescent seems to shift around at different latitudes. For dates far into the future, check this website: www.lunaroutreach.org/phases/phases.cgi

Acknowledgements

The publisher wishes to thank several people for commenting on parts of the manuscript in draft, and for various other kinds of support; many improvements were made as a result of their comments, but any flaws that may remain are our responsibility. Thanks are due to: Nick Anstead, Travers Cox, Andy Cronin, Dr Carol Darwin, M.B., B.Chir., Dr Maggie Eisner, Caroline Phillips, Brian Spence, Chris Thurman and Len Adam. Above all, heartfelt thanks to all the guides and porters without whom neither of the author's ascents would have been either possible or enjoyable.

Photo credits

Nick Anstead (p 32 lower), Michèle Cook (p 30, p 32 upper, p 37 upper, p 42 and p 59), Travers Cox (p 31 upper), Rob McSporran (p 6), anon (p 34 upper and 35 middle); all of the foregoing © Explore Worldwide and reproduced with its kind permission; Peter Blackwell/BBC Natural History Unit (p 60); Craig Smith (p 46); all other images © Jacquetta Megarry.

Index